Iraq

Charlie Samuels

Sarah Shields and Shakir Mustafa, Consultants

NATIONAL GEOGRAPHIC

WASHINGTON, D.C.

Contents

Foreword

raq's history has been a record of unsettling changes. In the past fifteen years alone, it has witnessed two major wars, crippling international sanctions, a foreign occupation, insurgency, and relentless terrorism. Iraq nonetheless is the land where a succession of cultures—Sumerian, Babylonian, Assyrian, and Abbasid—left many stamps of greatness, not only on the country itself but also on much of the surrounding region. Writing made its first appearance there, and so did the first set of civilized laws and the first documented collection of cooking recipes. The cradle of civilization, as Iraq is known, has been rocked too frequently, and too violently at times, but perhaps it is the drama in its history that has brought Iraq its numerous illustrious legacies.

The country is one of the most diverse in the Middle East: Arabs, Kurds, Turkmen, Assyrians, Mandaeans, and Armenians, among others, speak their own languages and retain their cultural and religious identities. Central to Iraqi culture is a vision of this pluralistic heritage as a source of energy for a better present and future. In facing the challenges of a demanding global culture, Iraqis are learning to look beyond the carnage of war and terror to build a democracy in which various communities participate regardless of ethnicity, religion, or ideological positions.

One of the virtues of this book is that it offers readers opportunities to know Iraqi history, culture, and people, and it relates that knowledge to current events. Discussion of sectarian divides, for instance, should help in understanding the present dangers of a civil war, and comments on the oppressive policies of the Hussein regime must shed light on Iraqis' continuing struggle to move beyond the country's dark legacy. Iraqis have

always viewed their history with a mixture of pride and pain. The
Baghdad of the Arabian Nights was for five centuries a beacon of
enlightenment to the rest of the world, but it appears unrelated to
today's city. The land's future will hang in the balance for some time, but
its liberating spirit is on the rise.

▲ Iraqi Kurds take a
pleasure cruise on some
rafts on the Zab River
in northern Iraq.

Shakir Mustafa
Boston University

Countries of the World: Iraq

An Ancient Paradise

RAQ IS A YOUNG COUNTRY. It only took its current shape early in the 1900s. The country is dominated by two famous rivers: the Tigris and Euphrates. The two rivers flow southeast from the Turkish highlands across the Iraqi plains toward the head of the Persian Gulf. They provide the water for a fertile region, an area that has been known by many names over the centuries. In Arabic, it was known as Al-Jazirah, or "the island." The Greeks called it Mesopotamia, or "the land between the rivers." Many Christian scholars believe it was the Garden of Eden, where the Old Testament said God created Adam and Eve, the first humans. Archaeologists have not found any trace of the biblical paradise, but Iraq did play an important role in early human history.

◀ Young men enjoy a swim in a river on a hot day in Baghdad. Shorts or bathing trunks are not acceptable among Muslims, so swimmers wear long pants.

WHAT'S THE WEATHER LIKE?

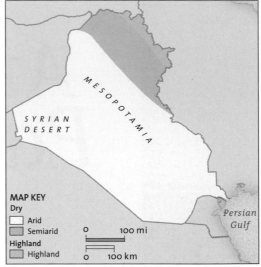

Much of Iraq has a desert climate, with mild or cool winters and hot dry summers when there is barely a cloud in the sky. Winters are far colder in the mountainous north of the country, along the borders with Turkey and Iran. These highlands sometimes get heavy winter snow. In the spring the snowmelt swells the rivers that sweep across the central plains, causing floods even in places that have seen almost no rain. Labels on this map and on similar maps throughout this book identify most of the places pictured in each chapter.

Fast Facts

OFFICIAL NAME: Republic of Iraq

FORM OF GOVERNMENT: Parliamentary democracy

CAPITAL: Baghdad

POPULATION: 26,783,383

OFFICIAL LANGUAGES: Arabic, Kurdish

MONETARY UNIT: New Iraq dinar (NID)

AREA: 168,754 square miles (437,072 square kilometers)

BORDERING NATIONS: Iran, Jordan, Kuwait, Saudi Arabia, Syria, Turkey

HIGHEST POINT: unnamed, 11,847 feet (3,611 meters)

LOWEST POINT: Persian Gulf, 0 feet (0 meters)

MAJOR RIVERS: Tigris, Euphrates

Average Temperature & Rainfall

Average High/Low Temperatures; Yearly Rainfall

BAGHDAD
86.5° F (30.3° C)/58.5° F (14.7° C); 5.5 in (14 cm)

BASRA
86.9° F (30.5° C)/63.9° F (17.7° C); 7.4 in (19 cm)

KIRKUK
71.1° F (21.7° C) (temperature year round); 15.8 in (40 cm)

MOSUL
67.8° F (19.9° C) (temperature year round); 15.2 in (39 cm)

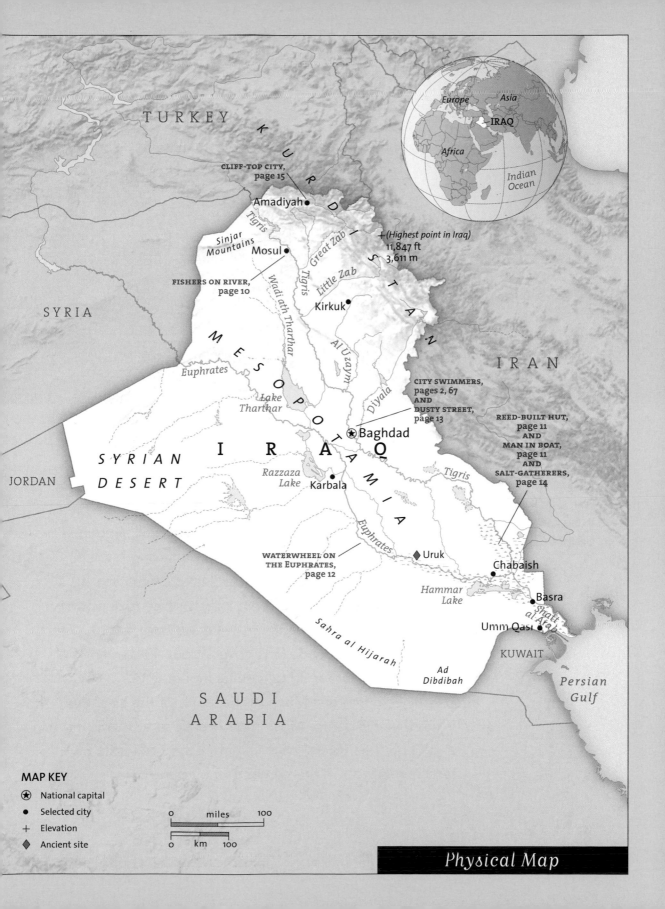

TURKEY

K U R D I S T A N

CLIFF-TOP CITY,
page 15

Amadiyah

Sinjar
Mountains

Tigris

Great Zab

Mosul

Little Zab

+ (Highest point in Iraq)
11,847 ft
3,611 m

FISHERS ON RIVER,
page 10

Tigris

Wadi ath Tharthar

Al Uzaym

Kirkuk

SYRIA

M
E
S
O
P
O
T
A
M
I
A

Euphrates

IRAN

Lake
Tharthar

Diyala

CITY SWIMMERS,
pages 2, 67
AND
DUSTY STREET,
page 13

REED-BUILT HUT,
page 11
AND
MAN IN BOAT,
page 11
AND
SALT-GATHERERS,
page 14

★ Baghdad

JORDAN

S Y R I A N
D E S E R T

I R A Q

Razzaza
Lake

Karbala

Tigris

Euphrates

WATERWHEEL ON
THE EUPHRATES,
page 12

Uruk

Chabaish

Basra

Hammar
Lake

Shatt
al Arab

Sahra al Hijarah

Umm Qasr

KUWAIT

Ad
Dibdibah

Persian
Gulf

SAUDI
ARABIA

Europe   Asia

IRAQ

Africa

Indian
Ocean

MAP KEY

★ National capital

● Selected city

+ Elevation

◆ Ancient site

0   miles   100

0   km   100

▲ Fishers cast their nets in the Tigris River in front of the old port city of Mosul, known as "the Pearl of the North" for its beautiful white buildings.

Paradise Lost

About seven thousand years ago the plains that make up about a third of Iraq were home to some of the world's first civilizations. Empires rose and fell there while people in Europe and the Americas still lived in rough shelters, hunting animals and gathering plants. Historians call Iraq one of the cradles of civilization.

Modern Iraq does not seem a likely place to support great empires. Many parts of the country are harsh places to live. Rocky deserts cover about 40 percent of the land. Another 30 percent is mountainous, with bitterly cold winters. Much of the south of the country is marshy and damp. Most Iraqis live close to the Tigris and Euphrates Rivers, which create a strip of fertile land running down the center of the country.

Rivers Flow

In ancient times, the Tigris and Euphrates flowed directly into the Persian Gulf. The gulf was a key route to the Indian Ocean and the east coast of Africa. However, over the centuries the rivers carried tons of silt down from the highlands and plains. They deposited the silt at the coast to form new land. Iraq's coastline is miles farther south now than it was in ancient times.

Today, the rivers join near the southern city of Basra to create a waterway called the Shatt al Arab. The eastern bank of the Shatt al Arab belongs to Iraq's neighbor, Iran. The two countries fought a war in the 1980s that left the waterway full of about 280 sunken ships.

▲ To irrigate palm groves, a waterwheel on the Euphrates uses the power of the current to lift water 30 feet (9 m).

▼ Dates can be eaten fresh, like this one, or dried, as they often are in the West.

Fertile Farmland

Iraq's central plains produce most of the country's food. Water is pumped out of the rivers and onto fields. Farmers grow wheat and corn, but the main crop is dates. Iraqis claim that a narrow strip on their side of the Shatt al Arab is the best area in the world for growing dates. At the start of the growing season, the dates are yellow and crunchy. Later in

the year, they are soft and brown. More than 500 varieties of date grow in Iraq, but date farmers say that they can tell the exact tree a date comes from, just from its taste.

▲ The heads of a clan of Marsh Arabs drink tea in a *mudhif*, or tribal house, built from reeds. Reeds are traditionally used for construction on soft, marshy land, because they are lighter than stone.

Flooded Land

In the very south of Iraq, the river water feeds huge areas of marshland and swamp. The marsh water gradually empties in the sea along the south coast. The marshes are filled with muddy islands and areas of thick reeds, and they are crisscrossed with a maze

LIFE IN THE MARSHES

People whose ancestors followed the same lifestyle for thousands of years live in the marshes in southern Iraq. The Ma'dan or Marsh Arabs lived by fishing and raising water buffalo or by growing rice and wheat. Until the 1970s, they tied and wove reeds together to make boats and to build homes with elaborate arched doorways. Similar homes are shown in a drawing from Uruk made five thousand years ago.

In the 1980s and 1990s Iraqi dictator Saddam Hussein drained the marshes to punish anti-government rebels hiding there. The number of people living in the marshes fell from 250,000 in 1991 to about 20,000. Today, about half of the land has been flooded

▲ A man paddles a boat through a marsh near Chabaish.

again, but some of the Marsh Arabs have changed their lifestyles for good. They live in brick homes and have community services, such as schools, hospitals, and running water, which are unavailable in the marshes. Even those who still fish have become more modern: They use motors on their boats, and their nets are wired to stun fish with electric shocks.

LOOK OUT, DUST!

In the spring and summer, the Shamal wind picks up dust from the desert and blows it in clouds toward cities. Baghdad may have up to five dust storms in July. Everyone ties scarfs or wet towels around their mouths. Drivers keep cleaning their windshields, but they still find it hard to see ahead. There are always more traffic accidents during a dust storm. Flights are cancelled and dust gets into machinery, causing electrical outages and crashing computer networks. Many people stay indoors, but even they do not escape. The dust gets in through cracks around doors and windows.

▲ After a storm, a Baghdad street is coated with brown dust from the desert.

It gets into food and drinking water. People complain of always having the taste of sand in their mouths. During storms, more people go to the hospital complaining of asthma or other breathing problems.

of hundreds of shallow waterways. Most land in the marsh is too damp and soggy to support heavy brick buildings. There are few roads, and the people of the marshes must travel everywhere by boat.

The Desert

In the west of Iraq, desert stretches all the way into Syria. Only a few scrubby plants can grow there. Few people live in the desert, but everyone knows that it is close by. There is no escape from the hot, dry wind called the Shamal, which blows dust from the deserts into the cities. Clouds of dust spread over Iraq and into neighboring countries. From space, the dust storms look like huge brown flowers in bloom.

THE SALT FLATS

Iraq's marshes covered an area twice as large as the Everglades in Florida before the 1990s, when they were drained by Saddam Hussein. As the marshes fill with water again, Western experts are eager to see the changes. It is difficult for them to get into Iraq, however. Most Iraqi experts have been isolated since the 1990s.

The northern marsh seems to be recovering well. Its clean water encourages plants to grow and fish to breed. The central marshes, however, have become salt flats. As water evaporates, it leaves salt and other minerals behind. They become more concentrated in what water is left and in the ground. Eventually there is so much salt that it is difficult for any animals or fish to survive. The salt flats are one of the world's harshest environments.

◀ The creation of the salt flats is not a disaster for everyone: These men are collecting salt to sell.

▼ Girls follow their camels through the desert, which is home to traditional nomads.

Land of the Kurds

Northeast of the Tigris Valley the land rises to high mountain ranges. The upper slopes are home to some of Iraq's only forests. Shortage of wood is one reason

that mud brick has always been the most important building material on the plains. The highlands have rich deposits of oil, with many oil wells and refineries. This part of the country is a long way from Baghdad, and transportation is difficult. In the winter, heavy snow blocks roads. In bad winters, people die from the cold. When the snow melts, floods wash away roads or cause landslides that block them.

The people of the highlands are different from the Arab Iraqis who live in the plains. They are Kurds, with their own history and languages, although many also speak Arabic. Kurds live in neighboring Turkey, Syria, and Iran as well. The Kurds from all these countries share an ambition to create their own independent nation named Kurdistan.

▲ The Kurdish city of Amadiya perches on top of cliffs near the Turkish border in northern Iraq. Many Kurds do not approve of the border. They believe that they all inhabit one region, Kurdistan.

Living on the Edge

ACCORDING TO LEGEND, THE WIND scorpion of Iraq's deserts runs faster than a man and screams like baby. Also known as a camel spider, it is said to crawl into camels' stomachs and eat them from the inside. In fact, the scorpion is silent. It is not even a scorpion but a relative of spiders. However, it can run very fast, hitting speeds of 10 miles an hour (16 km/h) as it scuttles for cover. The scorpion's name suggests how frightening it looks. Its immense jaws make up a third of the length of its body. They are used to slice up its victims, which include insects and lizards.

Iraq's deserts are a harsh environment. Animals are always on the lookout for water or food. In other Iraqi landscapes, animals have also had to adapt to demanding conditions.

◄ **The wind scorpion looks like it has ten legs, not eight as spiders and other scorpions have. However, the first pair are really feelers, not legs.**

PROTECTION NEEDED

It is a big job to protect Iraq's wildlife. There are effectively no protected natural areas in Iraq today. The government is concentrating on protecting people and property, rather than the natural world. But groups outside Iraq, such as the International Union for the Conservation of Nature (IUCN) have identified habitats that should be protected. They include places such as Iraq's marshes, which are used by migrating waterbirds. It is unlikely that habitat will be protected in the near future. However, almost a quarter of Iraq is habitat on which people have had almost no impact. Parts of the deserts and the high mountains still have largely undisturbed populations of native plants and animals.

▶ **Wolves were once common predators in Iraq, but they have been hunted by farmers to prevent them from stealing valuable livestock.**

Species at Risk

The precise status of some of Iraq's animals is uncertain. Before the invasion of 2003, the following species were classified as being at risk:

> Cheetah
> Dugong (mammal)
> Eurasian otter
> Lesser horseshoe bat
> Long-fingered bat

> Mehely's horseshoe bat
> Sind bat
> Smooth-coated otter
> Wild goat

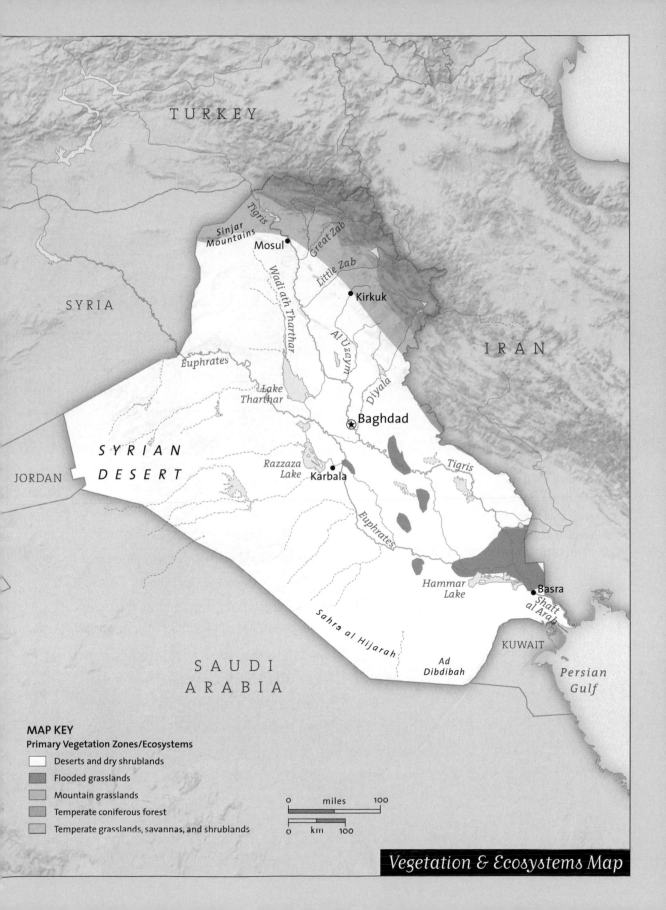

TURKEY

SYRIA

Sinjar
Mountains

Tigris

Mosul

Great Zab

Little Zab

Kirkuk

Wadi ath Tharthar

Al Uzaym

Euphrates

IRAN

Lake
Tharthar

Diyala

Baghdad

Tigris

Razzaza
Lake

Karbala

JORDAN

S Y R I A N
D E S E R T

Euphrates

Hammar
Lake

Basra

Shatt
al Arab

Sahra al Hijarah

Ad
Dibdibah

KUWAIT

SAUDI
ARABIA

Persian
Gulf

MAP KEY

Primary Vegetation Zones/Ecosystems

Deserts and dry shrublands

Flooded grasslands

Mountain grasslands

Temperate coniferous forest

Temperate grasslands, savannas, and shrublands

0   miles   100

0   km   100

Vegetation & Ecosystems Map

▲ The millions of locusts in a swarm make short work of destroying crops and other plants.

Out of the Deserts

When the skies above Iraq's deserts darken, the cause is often a sandstorm. But on rare occasions the low cloud has another cause. As it moves closer, people rush inside and shut their doors and windows. This cloud is a swarm of desert locusts, large grasshopper-like insects. Locusts usually live alone, but for reasons that no one really understands, they sometimes form swarms of about 40 to 80 million insects. They travel up to 80 miles (130 km) a day, stripping fields of crops. They occur from Africa as far east as India. The last major swarm to pass through Iraq and the Middle East occurred between 1987 to 1989.

Forest Life

The forests in the high mountains include firs that shed heavy snow in winter. On many of the slopes the trees have been cut down, but where the land is too steep for logging, the wild vegetation is still intact. Thorny shrubs grow on the forest floor, and wild daffodils and irises bloom in spring. In the hot, dry summers, there are frequent forest fires. They usually begin when lightning strikes a tree. Some pines have adapted to take advantage of the blazes. They do not drop their seed-bearing cones until a fire in the undergrowth covers the ground with a layer of ash. The carbon in the burned material helps to fertilize the pine seeds.

▲ In spring, blue irises are a common sight in Iraq's northern forests.

A Welcome Sanctuary

The forests in the northern highlands have largely been cut down. Only about four percent still stand. Oak trees grow near the snowline, and at lower levels there are food plants, including pistachio, almond, and walnut trees, and pear and hackberry trees. The forest remnants have survived because they are very remote. Although they are small,

THE LICORICE PLANT

One of Iraq's distinctive plants is licorice, a tall shrub with blue or violet flowers. Its yellow-brown roots are crushed to extract a juice used as a flavoring in cooking. It also makes a popular candy. The plant has been used for thousands of years for its health effects. Supplies were buried in the tomb of the ancient Egyptian king Tutankhamun, so that he had licorice for the afterlife. Warriors in ancient armies found that chewing it could stop them from getting thirsty on long marches. Today it is used to reduce stomach pain and to prevent swelling in arthritis sufferers.

▲ An Iraqi couple checks beehives in their orchard for honey. For 5,000 years, Iraqis have been keeping bees that collect pollen from wildflowers. Honey is an important source of food and income for many Iraqi families.

they are an important sanctuary for rare animals that retreated here to avoid contact with humans. They include wild sheep, brown bears, lynxes, leopards, and hyenas.

From Grasslands to Deserts

At lower elevations north of Kirkuk, the forest blends into steppe, or grassland. Most land is used for growing crops or for grazing goats and sheep. Damp areas near the rivers are home to thickets of poplar, tamarisk, and willow. Larks fly among the trees, filling the air with their song. The grasslands are home to a few wolves, which hunt badgers, gazelles, and hares. Even though they are so rare, shepherds still shoot the wolves, which sometimes take animals from flocks.

Farther south, the steppe fades into a scrubby shrub desert that marks the start of the true desert. People use camels to carry loads and to provide meat, milk, and wool. Streams and pools in the region often have water from November to March, when they support sagebrushes and salt trees.

Water and Marsh

Throughout Iraq, the rivers have plentiful fish, including giant members of the carp family that weigh up to 300 pounds (135 kg). Saltwater fish also swim in the rivers. In the 1950s, a bull shark swam from the Indian Ocean through the Persian Gulf and up the Tigris. Its dark fin was spotted at Baghdad. In the past, these man-eaters were said to attack Iraqis swimming at Basra.

▲ A boy stands poised to spear a fish in the Iraqi marshes. Fish are an important part of the Iraqi diet.

Iraqis depend on both the Tigris and the Euphrates to make sure they can grow enough food. Every bit of land that can be cultivated is covered in crops. Some of the marshlands in the south have been drained to provide more fertile land.

Land
of
Empires

I N ANCIENT IRAQ, MUD was not just dirt. It was the basis of empires. People cut mud from the banks of the Tigris and Euphrates and dried it in the sun to make bricks. Those bricks built some of the first cities anywhere. And mud made possible the invention of writing. The Sumerians of ancient Iraq wrote on tablets of clay that then hardened. The tablets have lasted better than the cities, whose bricks have worn away. The written records show that Iraq was already wealthy and powerful. Over thousands of years, many peoples were attracted by the region's resources and important position on land and water routes. They all left behind traces of their presence. Modern Iraq's diverse religions, peoples, and lifestyles are as much a record of its history as any bricks or clay tablets.

◄ **This restored ziggurat shows how it looked when it was built 4,000 years ago. Such huge structures required thousands of workers—and millions of bricks.**

FIRST PEOPLES

The first civilizations emerged on the plain of the Tigris and the Euphrates around 5000 B.C. The peoples who appeared in the following centuries are known as Sumerians. Sumer was a collection of city-states, some of which at times achieved power over the others. In Uruk, which was dominant from around 3600 to 2900 B.C., potters first used wheels to throw pots, and builders raised huge platforms to hold temples and other religious buildings. It was in Uruk that the first writing appeared. The writing was based on characters known as pictograms, images that resembled the objects they stood for. Within a few centuries, scribes were using only symbols rather than pictures, just as we do today. But the writing was not like ours. It was made up of lines known as cuneiform.

Cuneiform was the main form of writing in the region for about 3,000 years. Today, thousands of cuneiform tablets are historians' main clues about life in ancient Iraq.

▲ Cuneiform writing—cuneiform means "wedge-shaped"—was pressed into soft clay tablets with a wedge-shaped stick.

Time line

This chart shows the approximate dates for some of the major peoples who dominated ancient Mesopotamia. Many rulers were native to the region; others were invaders.

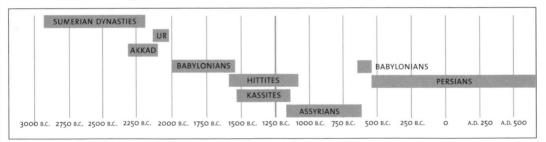

SUMERIAN DYNASTIES														
			UR											
		AKKAD												
			BABYLONIANS						BABYLONIANS					
				HITTITES						PERSIANS				
				KASSITES										
						ASSYRIANS								
3000 B.C.	2750 B.C.	2500 B.C.	2250 B.C.	2000 B.C.	1750 B.C.	1500 B.C.	1250 B.C.	1000 B.C.	750 B.C.	500 B.C.	250 B.C.	0	A.D. 250	A.D. 500

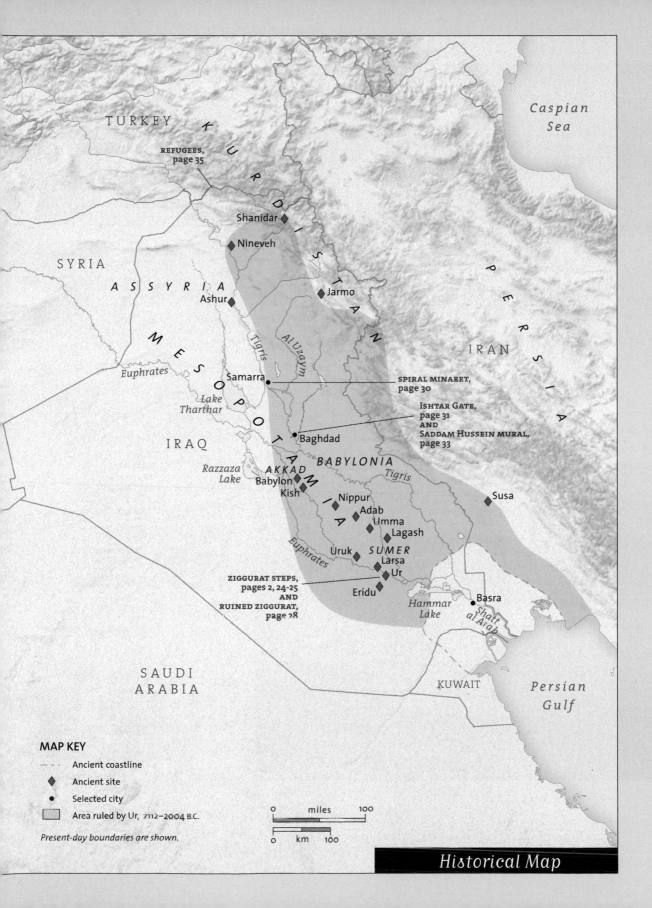

Caspian
Sea

TURKEY

K U R D I S T A N

REFUGEES,
page 35

Shanidar ◆

Nineveh ◆

SYRIA

A S S Y R I A

Ashur ◆

Jarmo ◆

M E S O P O T A M I A

Euphrates

Tigris

Al Uzaym

P E R S I A

IRAN

Lake
Tharthar

Samarra ●

SPIRAL MINARET,
page 30

ISHTAR GATE,
page 31
AND
SADDAM HUSSEIN MURAL,
page 33

IRAQ

Baghdad ●

B A B Y L O N I A

Tigris

Razzaza
Lake

A K K A D

Babylon ◆
Kish ◆

M I A

Nippur ◆

Adab ◆
Umma ◆
Lagash ◆

Susa ◆

Uruk ◆

S U M E R

Larsa ◆
Ur ◆

Euphrates

ZIGGURAT STEPS,
pages 2, 24-25
AND
RUINED ZIGGURAT,
page 28

Eridu ◆

Hammar
Lake

Basra ●

Shatt
al Arab

SAUDI
ARABIA

KUWAIT

Persian
Gulf

MAP KEY

– – – Ancient coastline

◆ Ancient site

● Selected city

▢ Area ruled by Ur, 2112–2004 B.C.

Present-day boundaries are shown.

miles

0   100

km

0   100

Historical Map

Rise and Fall

Sumer and other cities rose and fell. King Sargon of Akkad first united Mesopotamia in the 2300s B.C. He created an empire that stretched into Syria. The Akkadians ruled for nearly 150 years.

▲ A scene from one of the world's first epic poems. *Gilgamesh* told of the adventures of a Sumerian king.

▼ Goats graze in front of a ziggurat at Ur worn away by centuries of wind and rain.

Around 2000 B.C., one of the most famous Mesopotamian peoples rose to power: the Babylonians. Under King Hammurabi, the once-minor town of Babylon established a state covering southern Mesopotamia. The king introduced strong government based on a system of laws that laid out punishments for a range of crimes. Babylon's first period of power ended in 1595 B.C., when the city was overthrown by Hittites from the north.

Meanwhile the Assyrians had founded a trading empire in northern Mesopotamia and the Anatolian peninsula (modern Turkey) that dominated Iraq for 500 years. Assyria's rulers left descriptions of their deeds on monuments. Most of the kings themselves could not read or write. One of the last Assyrian rulers, Ashurbanipal, was so proud that he could read that he boasted about it on one of his monuments.

In the late seventh century the Assyrians were overthrown by the new rulers of Babylon. The Babylonian king Nebuchadrezzar led many military campaigns to increase the empire and built huge new buildings in the city. They included a system of rooftop terraces full of plants that became fabled as the Hanging Gardens of Babylon.

Successive Rulers

The end of Babylon came in 539 B.C., when Persians took over the city. In A.D. 646 invaders from Arabia finally overthrew the mighty Persian empire. The Arab conquerors left a lasting mark on Iraq by introducing the Islamic religion. Little more than a century later, the Abbasid dynasty founded Baghdad as the seat of the caliph, the spiritual leader of Islam. It became the leading city in the Islamic world and

TELLING THE FUTURE

The Babylonians were skilled at sciences, particularly at math and astronomy. They invented fortune-telling by the position of patterns of stars, called constellations. Their predictions were the origin of the horoscopes that are still popular in magazines. They also sacrificed goats and studied the animals' organs for signs. One scribe wrote on a tablet, "If the lobe of the liver is bright red and extends to the left, then the Elamites will be defeated."

▼ Ashurbanipal kills a lion in this scene of the king's hunting trip, which was carved in the seventh century B.C.

was full of scholars, scientists, and artists.

In A.D. 1258 the Mongols attacked from Central Asia and devastated Baghdad. The city would never regain its former glory. The region then came under the rule of the Turkish Seljuks.

Split Religion

In A.D. 1501 most of Iraq became part of Persia once more. The rest was ruled by the Ottomans, who had a large empire centered on Turkey. Islam is split into two branches, Shiites and Sunnis, with small but deep differences. The Iraqis living in Persia (now called Iran) became Shiite. Those under the Ottomans were Sunni.

▲ Pilgrims to the spiral minaret at Samarra must overcome any fear of heights. The ramp to the top has no safety rail.

Although today Sunni Muslims are in a majority in the world, Shiites are still the majority in Iraq and Iran. Iraq is home to the most important Shiite holy sites. Millions of pilgrims visit them each year.

Not all Iraqis are Muslim; there are also Christians and a few Jews. Iraq is also home to the Mandaeans, a group that follows the teachings of John the Baptist.

Empires of the West

The Ottomans conquered Iraq in A.D. 1534 and began a new period of peace. They centralized power in their capital, Istanbul. Baghdad remained a quiet and poor city until the late 1800s, when the Ottoman governor Midhat Pasha began to modernize the city. He built a water-supply system and the first bridge over the Tigris. Meanwhile, more Europeans were arriving in Iraq. The British built a coal storage facility near Basra to power steamships on the rivers. They wanted to increase trade but also to have a base to help guard the sea route through the Indian Ocean at the bottom

ANCIENT SYMBOL

German archaeologists working at Babylon in the 1900s discovered the ruins of the Ishtar Gate, a ceremonial entrance in the city walls. The gate was decorated with images of bulls and dragons, which were sacred to the goddess Ishtar. The bright colored tiles must have made a striking impression on visitors reaching the great city. The Germans built a replica of the Ishtar Gate in a museum in Berlin, Germany. Saddam Hussein later ordered a replica built in Iraq, to encourage national pride.

▶ The replica of the Ishtar Gate in Babylon is only half the size of the original.

▲ When his father died in 1933, Faisal II, age four, became king of Iraq. His uncle ruled in his place until he turned 18.

of the Persian Gulf to their colony in India.

An Arab State

In the early 20th century, a nationalist movement grew among the Iraqis. Supporters of this movement wanted the area around the Tigris and Euphrates Rivers to be an independent nation, ruled by Iraqis in Baghdad, not Istanbul. In World War I (1914–1918), however, the British occupied the region while they were fighting against the Turkish Ottoman Empire, and stayed after the war was over.

In 1920 nationalists in Iraq revolted against the British. The British offered the crown of Iraq to King Faisal I, brother of the king of Jordan. Faisal I was crowned in 1921. Iraq became independent in 1932, although the British still had a big influence in the country. The new country was wealthy, because oil had been discovered that could be sold abroad. But Iraq was not very stable. Politicians competed for power by creating uprisings among various Iraqi tribes. The army seized power in a coup in 1936.

When World War II began in 1939, the British were concerned that Iraq might decide to support their enemy, Germany, and supply them with valuable oil. British troops occupied Iraq again.

After the War

After the war ended in 1945, the region became important in the Cold War, the stand-off between the Western nations and the Communist nations, led by the Soviet Union. Both Britain and the United States had influence over Iraqi affairs. At the same time, nationalism became stronger in the Arab world. In 1948 the creation of Israel as a Jewish state angered Arabs who saw the land as their territory. And in Egypt, President Nasser became a hero among Arabs everywhere when he refused to accept any foreign governments having influence over his country.

In the late 1950s Iraq suffered from a period of coups. A new political party called the Baathists took power. The Baath Party believed Iraq should be ruled by Arabs. Saddam Hussein, a powerful member of the Baathists, took control of Iraq in 1979. Hussein ruled as a

▼ Several faces of Saddam Hussein appear on a mural in Baghdad. Images of the dictator were everywhere in Iraq because Hussein wanted Iraqis to identify him with the welfare of the nation.

NEIGHBORS AT WAR

Iraq and Iran once marked the border between the Arabic world and the Persian empire. They have often been hostile to each other. In 1980 Iraqi troops invaded Iran. Saddam Hussein wanted to control the whole of the Shatt al Arab waterway and take over Iran's oil-rich territory. The Iranians pushed the Iraqis back through the mid-1980s and occupied Iraqi land. Both sides bombed each other's cities. The Iraqis were criticized for using chemical weapons, and the Iranians for sinking Kuwaiti oil tankers in the Gulf. Many western countries that later turned against Hussein supported Iraq during the war. Up to 1.8 million people died before the United Nations arranged a cease-fire in 1988.

▲ Iraqi soldiers watch smoke rise from an Iranian port across the Shatt al Arab in 1981.

dictator, murdering or locking up opponents. His portrait was all over Iraq, and a holiday marked his birthday. Hussein favored his fellow Sunnis over the Shiites and the Kurds (who are not Arabs). In 1980 he led Iraq into a long war with neighboring Iran. In the north, Hussein tried to drive the Kurds out of areas with rich oil reserves. The Iraqi army used chemical weapons to kill hundreds of Kurdish civilians.

War and Crimes

In 1991 Hussein invaded the small neighboring state of Kuwait, to which Iraq had long laid claim. A U.S.-led coalition of many countries—including other Arab states, such as Syria—sent an army to stop him. The coalition quickly drove the Iraqi troops back into Iraq.

The Shiites and Kurds saw a chance to get rid of Hussein. But when they revolted, the coalition forces in Kuwait did nothing to help. Hussein punished the Shiites by draining the marshes at the heart of their region to ensure they remained poor and weak. The Kurds were forced from their homes by soldiers, and many fled across the border to Turkey.

The United Nations punished Iraq for invading Kuwait with sanctions. Iraq was banned from selling oil and buying products from abroad. The sanctions made ordinary Iraqis short of food and medicine. However, Hussein held on to power, and people became concerned that he was making more dangerous weapons with which to attack his own people and perhaps other countries. Despite objections from many other countries, the United States put together a new coalition. Its forces invaded Iraq in 2003 and took only a few days to fight their way to Baghdad. When they got there, Hussein had run away. The Baathist regime had come to an end—and yet another change of power in Iraq had begun.

▼ Kurdish refugees camp in the mountains of eastern Turkey after fleeing their homes in Iraq in 1991.

Tradition
and
Troubles

MOST PEOPLE GET ALONG with their cousins. They often play together as children. Sometimes they are really good friends. Traditionally in Iraq, more than half of all brides and grooms marry their first or second cousin. They argue that it makes good sense. The couple are likely to know each other well, or to share the same values. That should help them have a good marriage. Cousin-marriage also keeps property in the family. The family is the basis of Iraqi society— and it does not include only close relatives. The family includes everyone descended from the same ancestor. Members of these groups or tribes help each other, perhaps by finding jobs for people. Kinship is also an important influence on people's political opinions.

◀ A bride in Baghdad holds a copy of the Islamic holy book, the Koran, during her wedding party. Almost all Iraqis are Muslims.

A DIVIDED POPULATION

Most Iraqis are Arabs, although up to 20 percent are Kurds. Shiite Muslims make up about 65 percent of Iraqis, and Sunnis about 32 percent. About 3 percent of Iraqis follow the Christian faith. Until recently the gap between the branches of Islam has not been important. Members of the two groups often married, lived in the same parts of town, or came from the same clan. Today religion can be a matter of life and death. Both groups have been targeted by terrorists for their faith. And yet it is difficult to tell a Sunni and Shiite apart without knowing which mosque a person attends.

▶ Traffic is often congested in Baghdad, despite a recent decrease in the number of city dwellers.

Common Arabic Phrases

Nearly all Iraqis speak Arabic. Many also speak Kurdish, Farsi, and Turkmen. Arabic is spoken throughout much of North Africa and the Middle East. Most Arabic speakers can understand one another, although the pronunciation of words changes from country to country.

Salam alaikum (sa-LAM al-AY-kum)   Hello
Sabah al-khayr (sa-bah al-KAIR)   Good morning
Misa' al-khayr (mees-a' al-KAIR)   Good evening
Ma'as salama (MA'-as sa-LAM-ah)   Goodbye
Shukran (SHOO-kran)   Thank you
Afwan (ahf-waan)   You're welcome

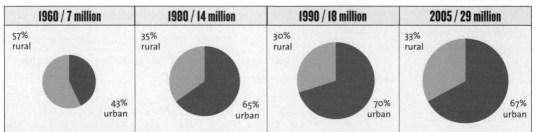

1960 / 7 million	1980 / 14 million	1990 / 18 million	2005 / 29 million
57% rural	35% rural	30% rural	33% rural
43% urban	65% urban	70% urban	67% urban

TURKEY

FAMILY PICNIC,
page 46
AND
ELECTION CELEBRATION,
page 47

Zakho

Dihok

Tall 'Afar

Mosul

Arbil

IRAN

SYRIA

Kirkuk

Sulaymaniyah

Chamchamal

WEDDING BRIDE,
pages 3, 36–37
AND
BUSY STREET,
page 38
AND
SHOPPING COUPLE,
page 40
AND
VIDEO GAMER,
page 41
AND
FAMILY MEAL,
page 44
AND
BOOK MARKET,
page 45

FERRIS WHEEL,
PAGE 42

Tikrit

Khanaqin

Samarra

Ba'qubah

Ramadi

Baghdad

Fallujah

SYRIAN
DESERT

Karbala

Musayyib

ORDAN

Hillah

Kut

PILGRIMS,
page 42

Kufah

Hayy

Najaf

Diwaniyah

Amarah

Shatrah

Samawah

Nasiriyah

Basra

Zubayr

MAP KEY

Population of urban area

▣ Over 1 million

▲ 250,000 to 1 million

● 100,000 to 250,000

• Under 100,000

SAUDI
ARABIA

KUWAIT

Persian
Gulf

People per square mile	People per square kilometer
Over 2500	Over 1000
250–2499	100–999
25–249	10–99
12.5–24	5–9
2.5–12.4	1–4
Under 2.4	Under 1

0   miles   100

0   km   100

Population Map

Simpler Celebrations

Iraqi weddings traditionally have many stages—and most involve a party. Families meet to check the ancestry of each partner before an engagement party. Before the wedding comes *nishan*, a big party with dancing to CDs or bands, and a small family ceremony called *Lailat al Henna*. The wedding day, too, has music and dancing—and there are still more parties to come. They are usually held on the fourth or seventh day after the wedding.

Today, couples often have smaller weddings. To show off their wealth might attract kidnappers. The parties used to go on into the night, but now they stop by 6:00 P.M., so that people can get home safely before dark.

▲ A couple shops for jewelry in Baghdad during their engagement. It is traditional for a groom to give his bride presents of gold before their wedding.

Dating Difficulties

Since the U.S.-led invasion of 2003, many young Iraqis find it difficult to date. It is hard to meet new friends because many people spend most of their time in their homes for safety. The restaurants where couples used to go on dates are empty. Some boys even call

random numbers on their cellphones in the hopes that a girl might answer. At school or college, religious groups try to persuade students that dating is a sin. Internet chat rooms are a popular way to meet other Iraqis, but one of the first questions is usually "Are you a Sunni or a Shiite?"

Marriages between Sunnis and Shiites were once common. Today, religious tensions make it harder for mixed couples. Some have divorced under pressure from their families. When Sunnis and Shiites do date, they often keep in touch secretly—by cellphone.

Musical Nation

The security situation means that there is less work now for the musicians who used to play at weddings. But Iraqi music is still highly respected. Baghdad's

▲ In an echo of the real violence in some parts of Iraq, a young Iraqi plays a combat game on his computer. Gaming is a popular pastime for boys and young men who spend long hours at home to avoid danger outside.

▲ Children ride on a
Ferris wheel to celebrate
Eid al-Fitr, the end of the
month of Ramadan, when
all Muslims fast during
the hours of daylight.

Institute of Fine Arts produced some of the most famous classical Arab musicians. Munir Bashir (1930–1997) introduced Arab music to audiences around the world. He was an outstanding player of the oud, or lute. Although the oud is used throughout the Arab world, only the Iraqis use it as a solo instrument.

In coffeeshops or at social events, people listen to *maqam*, a kind of song accompanied by a zither, an upright fiddle, and a drum. Everyone needs a lot of stamina, because a performance can last four hours. The singer sings a number of verses. Between each

PILGRIMS' PROGRESS

At Ashura, more than a million Shiites from all over Iraq travel to Karbala to mark the death of a seventh-century Shiite leader. The pilgrims wear black for mourning and smear themselves with dirt as a symbol of their grief. Some walk all the way from Baghdad, 60 miles (96 km) away, on bare feet. Others hurt themselves as a sign of the martyr's suffering, beating their chests or whipping or cutting their skin.

▶ Shiites wait to visit the Al-Abbas shrine in Karbala during the Ashura pilgrimage.

verse, the other performers sing a chorus to give him or her a chance to rest. Maqam is very popular. It drifts out of the doorways in coffeehouses in cities like Baghdad and Mosul.

Divided Nation

Iraqis once had some of the best schools and colleges in the Arab world. After the 1958 Baathist revolution, universities produced high numbers of scientists and other skilled workers. Many were women: In some years, more women graduated from college than men. Many went to study in the United States and Europe. That changed after the Gulf War in 1991 and the United Nations sanctions that followed. Many children quit school. They had to get jobs to boost the family income. There was little money for schools. Buildings were not repaired, and textbooks and equipment went out of date. The Baath Party told schools what they should teach.

Sadly, today only about 40 percent of Iraqis can read or write. Since the fall of Saddam Hussein, many schools have been rebuilt, but some parents are afraid to let their children attend. The journey to and from school can be scary in some cities, because of bombings

▼ A student reads from the blackboard in a traditional school in a rural village.

WOMEN IN BLACK

Women in Iraq traditionally had more freedom than in many countries in the region. They had jobs and could study; many had good jobs in government offices. They could wear Western style clothes, rather than Islamic traditional dress. Since the invasion, however, their situation has gotten worse. Religious groups try to force women to cover up. Some even threaten women wearing Western clothes. Many women wear the black sheet-like robe called an *abayah,* which covers their head and reaches to the floor.

▲ **Many women in Baghdad wear the traditional abayah.**

▼ **A family shares a meal in their home in Baghdad.**

and other violence. During vacations, many children are not allowed to go out to play. They stay indoors and watch satellite TV or play video games. Parents complain that their kids drive them crazy over the long summer break.

Ancient Dishes

Iraqi cooking reflects both Arabic and Persian influences. One Persian practice is the use of purple sumac flowers or rose petals in dishes. Iraq's national dish, *massgouf,* is made from a fish called *shabbut,* which is caught in the Tigris and served on a stick. The smell of barbecuing fish drifts from cafés along the river. Other favorite foods include dates, pomegranates, and eggplant. Some recipes that are still eaten today were written down thousands of years ago by cooks in ancient Babylon. Eggplant stew and honey-flavored pastry called baklava are still made from ancient recipes.

Traditionally all food in the home was prepared by women. Some dishes take many hours to get ready, such as chicken in fig sauce. When the food was ready, it was served to men in one room while the women ate in the kitchen. Modern urban families all eat together.

NAZIK AL-MALAIKA

The Iraqi Nazik al-Malaika is one of the most important and popular female poets in the Arab world. Her poems talk about the position of women in Iraqi society and about their role as the mothers of the country. Al-Malaika was born into a literary family in Baghdad in 1923, and began writing poetry early. Although she wrote in classical Arabic, she also experimented with modern forms of verse. She and her husband opened a university in the southern city of Basra. She also taught at the University of Kuwait for many years, until Iraqi troops invaded in 1990. Al-Malaika fled Iraq and settled in Cairo, Egypt, where she published a new collection of poems in 1999.

▼ **This street market in Baghdad sells nothing but books, many of which are in English.**

Literature

Iraq has a long literary tradition. In the tenth century, when Baghdad was the home of the caliph—the leader of the Islamic world—the city was a major cultural center. Today, Iraqi poets such as Badr Shakir al-Sayyab are popular among

THE BAGHDAD BLOGGER

Since the invasion of 2003, young Iraqis have used a new way to let people know what life in Iraq is like. Many started blogs on the Internet. One of the best-known was Salam Pax, a nickname made up of the words for "peace" in Arabic and Latin. Salam was a twenty-nine-year-old architect living with his parents in a suburb of Baghdad. He was frustrated that accounts of life in Iraq made it seem as if Iraqis were only interested in religion. He wanted to write about the things Iraqis did for fun. He also described how his family packed cases ready to flee their home, and how they watched the invasion on TV. Salam kept his identity secret for fear of attack by terrorists. Salam's lively posts showed a very different side to Iraqi life from regular news reports and were very popular. He was even invited by a British news program to make his own TV reports, which were shown around the world. He still makes TV reports about his life in Baghdad.

▼ A Kurdish family enjoys a picnic in a valley in northern Iraq. The Kurdish parts of the country are far more peaceful than the south.

Arabs. Al-Sayyab is most famous for a long poem he wrote in the 1950s. *Rainsong* is full of hope that Iraq will recover after centuries of decline.

Under Saddam Hussein, writers and other artists were expected to celebrate the state. Since Hussein's fall, writers have published more stories about daily life in Iraq, such as *Saddam City*, written by Mahmoud Saeed in 2004.

The written word is still a popular way for Iraqis to express their opinions. New newspapers are often printed by different Iraqi groups to express certain ideas. Most only last a few issues. Many people also post blogs on the

Internet. Every Friday Al Mutanabbi Street in Baghdad becomes the focus of Iraqi literary life. Writers and journalists gather in a café there to discuss Iraqi culture.

Kurdish Culture

Although Kurds can generally read Arabic, they have their own literature, as well as their own forms of music and architecture. Their popular epic poems are celebrations of the history of the Kurds. They inspire Kurds to look forward to a time when they are not divided by the borders of Iraq, Turkey, and other countries.

THE KURDS

For Kurds, the boundaries of Kurdistan are more important than the borders of Iraq, Iran, and Turkey that divide it. The Kurds were promised their own country after World War I, but the peace settlement ignored the promise. For the rest of the 20th century, the Kurds pushed for independence. Kurdish terrorists launched attacks in Turkey. The Iraqis attacked the Kurds during the Iran-Iraq War in the 1980s, and in the early 1990s Kurdish refugees fled to Turkey when the Iraqis drove them out. The Kurds celebrated (*below*) the fall of Hussein because they thought it made Kurdish independence more likely. The decals on this girl's cheek show the Kurdistan flag.

Up From
the
Ashes

I N 1991, THE IRAQI ARMY was forced out of Kuwait by soldiers from the United Nations coalition. As they retreated, the Iraqi troops set fire to Kuwait's desert oil wells. Soon black smoke filled the skies of southern Iraq, and the red glow from the burning oil could be seen from space. It took months to put out all the fires. The Iraqis also emptied Kuwait's oil into the Persian Gulf, creating the largest oil slick every seen, which was disastrous for the region's waterbirds and fish.

The war was also an economic disaster for Iraq, when U.N. sanctions blocked its oil trade. Iraq has the world's second largest supply of oil—about 11 percent of the world's total. Without the money raised by selling oil, Iraq rapidly became a poor country.

◀ **Oil wells burn in the Kuwaiti desert at the end of the Persian Gulf War in 1991. The fires were an environmental disaster as well as an economic setback.**

At a Glance

NEW DEMOCRACY

Iraqis voted in the country's first democratic elections for over 50 years in January 2005. The result of these elections were not simple, and it was another three months before an elected government could take office. The delay was caused by the concerns of the different groups living in Iraq: the Sunnis, Shiites, and Kurds. Under Hussein, the Sunnis had been in charge of Iraq. But most Iraqis are Shiites and with the Kurds they control most of the government. However, Iraq's new democracy is set up to ensure that every Iraqi group is involved in the way the country is run.

Trading Partners

Iraq's international trade was virtually halted during the 1990s, when the United Nations restricted trade as a punishment for the 1991 invasion of Kuwait. Since the 2003 invasion, trade has been held back by the security situation. Key industries have been damaged by attacks on facilities such as oil pipelines. Exports are mostly oil or oil-related products. The key imports are food, medicines, and manufactured goods.

Country	Percent Iraq exports
United States	49.3
Italy	10.3
Spain	6.2
All others combined	34.2

Country	Percent Iraq imports
Turkey	23.2
Syria	23.0
United States	11.6
All others combined	42.2

▼ Jalal Talabani, (*fourth from right*) speaks to reporters after becoming president of Iraq in April 2005.

TURKEY

38°N

DAHUK
Dahuk
(Dihok)

GRAZING SHEEP,
page 55

JALAL TALABANI,
page 50
AND
LOOTER,
page 53
AND
VOTER,
page 53
AND
SADDAM TRIAL,
page 54
AND
SOLDIER,
page 56
AND
DONNY GEORGE,
page 57

Mosul

ARBIL
Arbil

36°N

NINAWA
(NINEVEH)

SYRIA

Kirkuk
AT
TA'MIM

As Sulaymaniyah
AS
SULAYMANIYAH

IRAN

Tikrit

SALAH
AD DIN

DIYALA

34°N

Ba'qubah

Ramadi

BAGHDAD
Baghdad

JORDAN

SYRIAN
DESERT

AL ANBAR

Karbala
KARBALA

BABIL
Hillah

WASIT
Kut

32°N

Najaf

Diwaniyah
AL QADISIYAH

MAYSAN
'Amarah

AN NAJAF

Samawah

DHI QAR
Nasiriyah

Basra
AL BASRAH

AL MUTHANNA

30°N

SAUDI
ARABIA

BURNING OIL WELLS,
pages 3, 48–49

KUWAIT

Persian
Gulf

28°N

MAP KEY
⊛ National capital
◉ Governorate capital

miles

0   100

km

0   100

38°E   40°E   42°E   44°E   46°E   48°E

Political Map

In Transition

Since 2003, Iraq has been occupied by many thousands of U.S. troops and forces from other coalition countries. Some people believe that the troops are there to make sure that Western countries can control Iraq's oil—as happened in the early 1900s. However, the Iraqi government says that it needs the foreign troops to control the country while a new Iraqi army and police force are being built.

The 2005 elections allowed Iraqi politicians to take control of their country again after the fall of Saddam Hussein. The new Iraqi government took over from a series of temporary authorities, which had been run by

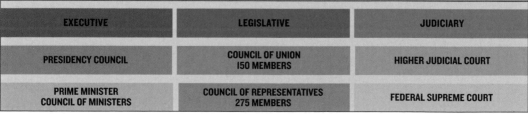

HOW THE GOVERNMENT WORKS

Under Iraq's new constitution, most power is held by the prime minister, Nouri al-Maliki, but the head of state is the president. In 2005, Jalal Talabani, a Kurd, became the first president. The two vice presidents were Tariq al-Hashimi, a Sunni, and Adel Abdul Mehdi, a Shiite. The government has a two-chamber parliament. The Council of Representatives has 275 members chosen in popular elections. The upper house, the Council of Union, includes fifty senators each to represent Shiites, Sunnis, and Kurds, to make sure that legislation does not favor one ethnic group over the others. The Iraqi court system has been restored since the fall of Saddam Hussein, but critics say that it is not working well.

PRESIDENT		
EXECUTIVE	LEGISLATIVE	JUDICIARY
PRESIDENCY COUNCIL	COUNCIL OF UNION 150 MEMBERS	HIGHER JUDICIAL COURT
PRIME MINISTER COUNCIL OF MINISTERS	COUNCIL OF REPRESENTATIVES 275 MEMBERS	FEDERAL SUPREME COURT

officials from both Iraq and coalition countries.

After the invasion the coalition disbanded the army and police force that served under Hussein. That left no one to keep order, and since then there has been widespread lawlessness in Iraq, which the coalition troops can do little to stop. Armed rebels, called insurgents, regularly attack coalition forces. They also target the new Iraqi police, who the insurgents resent for working with the "enemy"—the Americans and other foreign powers.

▲ A looter makes off with a luxurious couch after the 2003 invasion. When law and order broke down, looting became a widespread problem.

A Hard Task

The new Iraqi government faces severe problems. Iraq has enough oil and gas reserves to make it one of the richest countries in the world. However, its economy is in ruins after decades of costly wars and sanctions.

People have lost their jobs and live in poverty, with little food for their families.

The 2003 invasion gave the country an opportunity to

◀ A woman proudly displays the inked finger that shows that she has voted in the 2005 poll on the new constitution.

rebuild, but its problems got worse in many ways. The administrators in Hussein's government had lost their jobs. Government buildings were looted, and the country became chaotic. Hospital workers even had to steal the medical supplies needed to treat patients.

Roads, sewers, and water and power supplies had been very rundown and were damaged in the fighting. A huge reconstruction program was planned, to be paid for with foreign aid money and the profits from selling Iraq's oil. Many Iraqis hoped to get jobs rebuilding their country. Others offered to work for the new government, perhaps by joining the police force. However, that made them targets for the insurgents. Thousands of Iraqis have been killed just for trying to earn a living. It is still too dangerous in Iraq for many reconstruction projects to start, and the country is still in ruins years after Hussein was removed.

TRIAL OF A DICTATOR

Saddam Hussein was captured in December 2003. In 2006, he went on trial for crimes against humanity (*below*). Hussein insisted that the court was not legal. Other critics complained that it was under the influence of the United States, even though Hussein was tried by Iraqi judges under Iraqi law. He was found guilty and sentenced to death. Hussein was hanged on December 30, 2006.

Everyday Hardships

Now that the sanctions against Iraq have ended, people can buy modern products, such as TVs and refrigerators, which were not available under Hussein. But Iraqis

do not show off their new purchases: Someone with a new car and a nice home might attract kidnappers after a ransom.

New household goods are not much use when homes get only a couple of hours of electricity a day. Some families have generators to run air conditioners in summer, but fuel is in short supply. Drivers often sit in line at gas stations for a whole day to buy fuel.

▲ Shepherds herd their sheep on the green hills of northern Iraq. Goats and sheep are the main sources of meat in Iraq: Muslims are forbidden to eat pork.

Strained Resources

Iraq's farmers cannot feed all Iraqis, despite the use of irrigation to grow as many crops as possible. The principal crops are cereals—wheat, rice, corn, and barley—and fruits, cotton, and dates. In the 1980s and

THE WORLD'S HERITAGE

Iraq is home to sites built by some of the first civilizations, such as Uruk and Babylon. After the invasion of 2003, it became difficult to protect such sites against looters. Priceless treasures were also looted from the National Museum in Baghdad. Many later turned up again, but some are likely gone forever. The United States diverted military forces to protect some of the most important sites, but their protection will not last, and the valuable sites may again be under threat.

▲ A U.S. Marine looks out from a parapet over the ruins of ancient Babylon, which lie 50 miles (80 km) south of Baghdad.

1990s, many farmers left the land to look for work in the cities. Saddam's government destroyed many irrigation canals. Today, Iraq has to import food. Iraq's other natural resources include natural gas, used to produce energy, phosphates for making fertilizers, sulfur, and salt. Most factories are out of date, however, or have been damaged by wars. In the cities, business has suffered because of terrorist bombings and nightly curfews that stop people from going out.

A New Future

Life for many Iraqis remains hard, but there are some reasons for optimism. Agencies such as the United Nations and the United States Agency for International Development fund projects to restore the government departments and create jobs. They aim to improve sanitation, to reopen schools and train new teachers, and to build new hospitals. In Sulaymaniyah, cranes on the skyline mark ambitious building projects. In Najaf, tourists again visit holy shrines. Few foreign tourists will visit, however, until the country is much safer.

Many Iraqis have left the country, but most have no choice

but to stay and adapt to living with the dangers. Many believe that life will only improve when coalition troops leave Iraq. When that might be remains anyone's guess, but when it happens Iraqis will be ready. Their country has undergone many changes over the centuries. The Iraqi people have always proved resourceful at coping with change. When the final troops leave Iraq, a new generation of Iraqis will be set to make the most of whatever new situation faces them.

▲ **Donny George, director of the National Museum in Baghdad, shows off treasures recovered from looters. Such artifacts are a reminder of Iraq's former glory—and a sign of hope for the future.**

Government & Economy   **57**

Add a Little Extra to Your Country Report!

I f you are assigned to write a report about Iraq, you'll want to include basic information about the country, of course. The Fast Facts chart on page 8 will give you a good start. The rest of the book will give you the details you need to create a full and up-to-date paper or PowerPoint presentation. But what can you do to make your report more fun than anyone else's? If you use your imagination and dig a bit deeper into some of the topics introduced in this book, you're sure to come up with information that will make your report unique!

>Flag

Perhaps you could explain the history of Iraq's flag, and the meanings of its colors and symbols. Go to **www.crwflags.com/fotw/flags** for more information.

>National Anthem

How about downloading Iraq's national anthem, and playing it for your class? At **www.nationalanthems.info** you'll find what you need, including the words to the anthem, plus sheet music for the anthem. Simply pick "I" and then "Iraq" from the list on the left-hand side of the screen, and you're on your way.

>Time Difference

If you want to understand the time difference between Iraq and where you are, this Web site can help: **www.worldtimeserver.com**. Just pick "Iraq" from the list on the left. If you called Iraq right now, would you wake whomever you are calling from their sleep?

>Currency

Another Web site will convert your money into dinars, the currency used in Iraq. You'll want to know how much money to bring if you're ever lucky enough to travel to Iraq: **www.xe.com/ucc**.

>Weather

Why not check the current weather in Iraq? It's easy—simply go to **www.weather.com** to find out if it's sunny or cloudy, warm or cold in Iraq right this minute! Pick "World" from the headings at the top of the page. Then search for Iraq. Click on any city you like. Be sure to click on the tabs below the weather report for Sunrise/Sunset information, Weather Watch, and Business Travel Outlook, too. Scroll down the page for the 36-hour Forecast and a satellite weather map. Compare your weather to the weather in the Iraqi city you chose. Is this a good season, weather-wise, for a person to travel to Iraq?

>Miscellaneous

Still want more information? Simply go to National Geographic's One-Stop Research site at **http://www.nationalgeographic.com/onestop**. It will help you find maps, photos and art, articles and information, games and features that you can use to jazz up your report.

Glossary

Arab a person whose distant ancestors come from the Arabian Peninsula in southwest Asia.

Blog a personal diary or journal that is published for all to see on the World Wide Web.

Coalition a group of nations or organizations that works together to achieve certain goals.

Coup when military leaders take control of a country replacing the politicans. The full phrase is *coup d'etat*.

Epic poem a very long poem that tells the stories of heroes and legends.

Fast a period when a person decides not to eat, and perhaps drinks nothing, too.

Habitat a part of the environment that is suitable for certain plants and animals.

Irrigation taking water from a river or a well to use on fields and in plantations.

Kin a person's relatives.

Mesopotamia an old name for the land between and nearby to the Tigris and Euphrates Rivers.

Migration the annual movement of animals, such as birds, deer, or whales, from one place to another.

Millennium a period of one thousand years, or ten centuries.

Minaret the tower on a mosque, from which the faithful are called to prayer.

Native a person or species that is originally from a certain place.

Nomad a person who moves often, rather than living in one place.

Pilgrimage a journey made for religious reasons.

Refinery a factory where petroleum oil or another substance is purified into more useful products.

Regime a system by which a country is run. Also the group in power in a country.

Sanctions an international agreement that sets out a number of punishments against a country.

Sanctuary a place of safety.

Sediment the soil and dirt that settles on the ground. Sediment is generally dropped by wind or water.

Shiite a Muslim who follows the teachings of the twelfth imam.

Silt very fine soil and clay that is carried by large rivers. As it settles to the riverbed, silt forms deep mud.

Species a type of organism; animals or plants in the same species look similar and can only breed successfully among themselves.

Sunni the mainstream branch of Islam.

Swarm a large group of flying insects, generally bees or locusts.

United Nations (UN) an international organization that includes most of the countries of the world. The UN is where the world's governments discuss the world's problems and figure out how to work together.

Ziggurat a stepped pyramid built in Iraq and the surrounding region in ancient times.

Bibliography

Coleman, Wim. *Iraq in the News: Past, Present, and Future.* Berkeley Heights, NJ: MyReportLinks.com Books, 2006.

Hunter, Erica C. D. *Ancient Mesopotamia* (Cultural Atlases for Young People). New York: Facts on File, 2007.

Lightfoot, Dale. *Iraq.* New York: Chelsea House Publishers, 2007.

Sinkler, Adrian. *Nations in Transition: Iraq.* Farmington Hills, MI: Greenhaven Press, 2005.

Steele, Phillip. *Mesopotamia* (DK Eyewitness Books), New York: DK Children, 2007.

Tripp, Charles. *A History of Iraq.* Cambridge: Cambridge University Press, 2002.

http://www.arab.net/iraq/index.html
(general information about the country)

http://www.iraqigovernment.org/index-EN.htm
(government Web site)

http://news.bbc.co.uk/1/shared/spl/hi/in_depth/post_saddam_iraq/html/1.stm
(information about life in modern Iraq)

Further Information

NATIONAL GEOGRAPHIC Articles

Boulat, Alexandra. "Bagdhad Before the Bombs." NATIONAL GEOGRAPHIC MAGAZINE (June 2003): 52–69.

Lawler, Andrew. "Beyond the Looting: What's Next for Iraq's Treasures?" NATIONAL GEOGRAPHIC MAGAZINE (October 2003): 58–75.

Web sites to explore

More fast facts about Iraq, from the CIA (Central Intelligence Agency): https://www.cia.gov/cia/publications/factbook/geos/iz.html

Do you want to know more about Iraq's ancient history? Take a look at this site created by the British Museum: http://www.mesopotamia.co.uk/menu.html

Who are the Kurds? Find out from this online article: http://www.washingtonpost.com/wp-srv/inatl/daily/feb99/kurdprofile.htm

What is it like to be a Marsh Arab? Check out this charity that helps preserve the Marsh Arabs' way of life: http://www.amarappeal.com/marsh_arabs.php

See, hear

Because Iraq can sometimes be dangerous, it is difficult to get a taste of life there. You might be able to locate these movies and music CDs:

Kilometre Zero
A 2005 movie made by Iraqi director Hiner Saleem re-creates life in the country before the fall of Saddam Hussein and looks at relations between Arabs and Kurds.

My Country, My Country
A documentary made in Iraq by U.S. director Laura Poitras follows an Iraqi Sunni doctor running as a candidate in the January 2005 elections.

Turtles Can Fly
A Kurdish language film about villagers awaiting the 2003 U.S. invasion of Iraq.

Choubi Choubi! Folk and Pop Sounds from Iraq (2005)
A compilation of modern Iraqi music by different artists.

Index

Credits

Picture Credits

Front Cover – Spine: Robin Meredith/Shutterstock; Top: Michael S. Yamashita/Corbis; Low far left: Michael S. Yamashita/NGIC; Low left: Atef Hassan/Reuters/Corbis; Low right: Nik Wheeler/Corbis; Low far right: EPA/Corbis.

Interior – Corbis: Thaier Al-Sudani/Reuters: 53 lo; Archivo Iconografico, S.A.: 29 lo; Ceer Wan Aziz/Reuters: 22 up, 42 lo; Zohra Bensemra/Reuters: 3 left, 36–37; Bettmann: 28 lo, 32 lo; David Furst/POOL/EPA: 54 lo; Michael & Patricia Fogden: 2 right, 16–17; Shai Ginott: 18 lo; Ali Jasim/Reuters: 42 up; Ed Kashi: 44 lo, 46 lo, 55 up; Faleh Kheiber/Reuters: 40 center, 50 lo; Frans Lemmens/Zefa/: 20 up; Benjamin Lowry: 53 up; Francois de Mulder: 34 up; Namir Noor-Elden/Reuters: 47 lo; Stephani Sinclair: 57 up; Peter Turnley: 3 right, 35 lo, 48–49; Max Whittaker: 41 up; Michael S. Yamashita: 45 lo; Empics: Aleander Zemlianichenko: 56 up; NG Image Collection: Lynn Abercrombie: 10 up, 12 lo, 11 up, 13 lo, 14 lo, 15 up, 23 center, 26 center, 30 up, 31 lo, 33 up, 43 lo; Alexandra Boulat: 2 left, 6–7, 13 up, 14 up, 38 lo, 44 up; Dean Conger: 28 lo; Steve McCurry: 2–3, 24–25; Richard Olsenius: 21 up; Priit Vesilind: TP; Michael S. Yamashita: 5 up, 12 up; Shutterstock: Pilar Echevarria: 11 lo; Denise Sirois: 59 up.

For more information, please call 1-800-NGS-LINE (647-5463) or write to the following address:

NATIONAL GEOGRAPHIC SOCIETY
1145 17th Street N.W.
Washington, D.C. 20036-4688 U.S.A.

Visit the Society's Web site at www.nationalgeographic.com

Library of Congress Cataloging-in-Publication Data available on request
ISBN: 978-1-4263-0061-5

Printed in Belgium

Series design by Jim Hiscott.
The body text is set in Avenir; Knockout.
The display text is set in Matrix Script.

Front Cover—Top: Children ride on a Ferris wheel in Samarra; Low Far Left: The Khadimain Mosque in Baghdad; Low Left: Oil refineries; Low Right: Camels at a waterhole; Low Far Right: Fishers with nets in marshes near Karbala

Page 1—A fisherman in Basra; Icon image on spine, Contents page, and throughout: Detail of ancient building

Produced through the worldwide resources of the National Geographic Society

John M. Fahey, Jr., *President and Chief Executive Officer*; Gilbert M. Grosvenor, *Chairman of the Board*; Nina D. Hoffman, *Executive Vice President, President of Book Publishing Group*

National Geographic Staff for this Book

Nancy Laties Feresten, *Vice President, Editor-in-Chief of Children's Books*
Bea Jackson, *Director of Design and Illustration*
David M. Seager, *Art Director*
Virginia Koeth, *Project Editor*
Lori Epstein, *Illustrations Editor*
Stacy Gold, Nadia Hughes, *Illustrations Research Editors*
Carl Mehler, *Director of Maps*
Priyanka Lamichhane, *Assistant Editor*
R. Gary Colbert, *Production Director*
Lewis R. Bassford, *Production Manager*
Maryclare Tracy, Nicole Elliott, *Manufacturing Managers*

Brown Reference Group plc. Staff for this Book

Volume Editor: Sally MacEachern
Designer: Dave Allen
Picture Manager: Becky Cox
Maps: Martin Darlinson
Artwork: Darren Awuah
Index: Kay Ollerenshaw
Senior Managing Editor: Tim Cooke
Design Manager: Sarah Williams
Children's Publisher: Anne O'Daly
Editorial Director: Lindsey Lowe

About the Author

CHARLIE SAMUELS studied at the University of Oxford before beginning a career in publishing that has lasted over 20 years. He has written hundreds of articles and dozens of books for younger readers, particularly about historical and cultural subjects, and has also edited many reference encyclopedias. He lives in London, where his nephews and godchildren are happy to tell him how to be a better writer.

About the Consultants

DR. SARAH SHIELDS is a professor of history at the University of North Carolina, Chapel Hill. She is currently researching the development of national identities in the Middle East between the two world wars. Her book, *Mosul Before Iraq*, focuses on the economic history of northern Iraq during the last century of Ottoman rule. She has two children who have gotten used to traveling with her on research trips.

DR. SHAKIR MUSTAFA is Assistant Professor of Arabic at Boston University. His research focuses on Arabic, Muslim, and Irish literatures, and he has recently translated, introduced, and edited an anthology of Iraqi fiction to be published by Syracuse University Press. Professor Mustafa grew up in Iraq and taught at Baghdad and Mosul Universities.

Quoted in *Sumer: Cities of Eden* (Lost Civilizations). Alexandria, VA: Time-Life Books, 1993.

Time Line of
Iraqi History

ca 6000 Farming begins in the area that is now Iraq.

ca 3800 The Sumerians dominate the Iraq area from their major city, Uruk.

2300s Mesopotamia is united by King Sargon of Akkad.

ca 2000 The Babylonians rise to power; they reach their peak under Hammurabi from 1792 to 1750 .

1200s The Assyrians incorporate Mesopotamia as a province in their empire.

ca 600 Nebuchadrezzar builds the hanging gardens of Babylon for his wife, to remind her of the hills in her homeland, Persia, now Iran.

539 Cyrus, the new emperor of Persia, conquers Babylon and incorporates Iraq into the Persian Empire.

330 Alexander the Great captures Babylon from the Persians and attempts to make Babylon the capital of the world.

144 The Parthian Empire, a coalition of Central Asian tribes, capture Babylon and found their capital, Ctesiphon, south of modern-day Baghdad.

224 Persian invaders take control of Iraq and found the Sassanian Empire.

570 Birth of Muhammad, the founder and prophet of Islam.

646 Arabian Muslims overthrow the Persian empire in Mesopotamia.

762 Baghdad is founded and becomes the capital of a caliphate.

836 In response to attacks by the Ottoman Turks, the Abbasids move the caliphate from Baghdad to Samarra.

892 The Abbasid capital returns to Baghdad.

943 The Buyid, Shiites from Iran, capture Baghdad. The Buyid have effective control over Iraq for the next hundred years.

1000

1055 Seljuk Turks capture Baghdad; a Seljuk prime minister, Nizam ul-Mulk, establishes a series of colleges to train civil servants in Baghdad.

1200

1258 Mongol armies led by Hulagu capture Baghdad and massacre approximately 800,000 of its citizens.

1400

1401 The Mongol conquerer Tamerlane attacks Baghdad and kills 90,000 of its inhabitants.

1500

1534 Iraq is conquered by the Turks and incorporated into the Ottoman empire.

1700

1790s The British establish a consulate in Baghdad in order to protect communications with their colony, India.